OCT 2 3 2019

STEM
STORIES

Medicine

FROM HIPPOCRATES TO JONAS SALK

Jessie Alkire

Checkerboard
Library

An Imprint of Abdo Publishing
abdopublishing.com

ABDOPUBLISHING.COM

Published by Abdo Publishing, a division of ABDO, PO Box 398166, Minneapolis, Minnesota 55439. Copyright © 2019 by Abdo Consulting Group, Inc. International copyrights reserved in all countries. No part of this book may be reproduced in any form without written permission from the publisher. Checkerboard Library™ is a trademark and logo of Abdo Publishing.

Printed in the United States of America, North Mankato, Minnesota
052018
092018

THIS BOOK CONTAINS RECYCLED MATERIALS

Design and production: Mighty Media, Inc.
Editor: Liz Salzmann
Cover Photographs: AP Images (right), iStockphoto (left, middle)
Interior Photographs: Alamy, pp. 19, 29 (bottom); AP Images, pp. 23, 27; Imperial War Museum/Wikimedia Commons, pp. 17, 29 (top); iStockphoto, pp. 7, 11, 21; Science Museum, London, p. 14; Shutterstock, pp. 4–5, 15, 25; Wellcome Collection, pp. 9, 28 (top); Wikimedia Commons, pp. 13, 28 (bottom)

Library of Congress Control Number: 2017961643

Publisher's Cataloging-in-Publication Data
Name: Alkire, Jessie, author.
Title: Medicine: From Hippocrates to Jonas Salk / by Jessie Alkire.
Other titles: From Hippocrates to Jonas Salk
Description: Minneapolis, Minnesota : Abdo Publishing, 2019. | Series: STEM stories |
     Includes online resources and index.
Identifiers: ISBN 9781532115479 (lib.bdg.) | ISBN 9781532156199 (ebook)
Subjects: LCSH: Medicine--History--Juvenile literature. | Clinical sciences--Juvenile
     literature. | Medical profession--Juvenile literature. | Inventors--Biography--Juvenile
     literature.
Classification: DDC 610.922--dc23

Contents

Have you been to the doctor lately? Did the doctor ask any questions or run any tests? Did she ask about your **symptoms** and look into your throat or ears?

Medicine is the science of healing. It is the **diagnosis**, treatment, and prevention of diseases. It also focuses on the promotion of health. But medicine didn't always focus on these areas.

Medicine has a history that goes back to prehistoric times. Back then, people didn't know what caused diseases. They believed gods or spirits caused people to get sick. Scientific knowledge increased very slowly over hundreds of years.

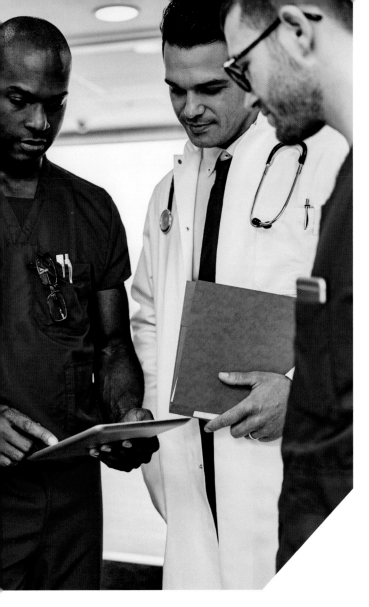

Teamwork is important in the medical field. Doctors, nurses, and other hospital staff work together to provide the best care for patients.

Medical advancements started occurring more quickly in the late 1800s. Scientists discovered new treatments, such as antibiotics and vaccines. They also invented x-ray machines and other tools that helped doctors treat patients.

Today's scientists and doctors continue to develop new drugs, instruments, and medical procedures. Diseases that carried a death sentence just decades ago are now treatable. But scientists think we can push further and find better treatments or even cures for many diseases.

CHAPTER 1

Early Medicine

The history of medicine goes back many thousands of years. Ancient people believed major diseases were caused by gods or other supernatural forces. The first doctors were known as medicine men or shamans. They were thought to be witches or sorcerers. Instead of using science and medicine, they tried to cure illnesses with potions and spells.

One procedure that ancient people practiced was trepanning. In trepanning, a hole was made in the skull. This process was thought to release the supernatural being causing the **symptoms**. Researchers have found many skulls that show evidence of trepanning. People may have lived for years after it was done to them!

Medical skills and practices varied according to region and religion. But by about 2000 BCE, doctors from Egypt to China had strong medical knowledge. Egyptian doctors had advanced knowledge of organs and bone structures. The Chinese used ginseng and other plants to treat illnesses.

Historians have learned much about ancient Egyptian medical practices from art. Drawings and carvings show medical tools including bone saws, hooks, needles, scissors, and knives.

As time went on, medicine shifted from supernatural to scientific. Ancient Greek philosophers drew on science to explain illness and create new treatments. The leading voice in Greek medicine was Hippocrates, also known as the Father of Medicine.

CHAPTER 2

Supernatural to Science

Hippocrates is a mysterious figure in history. Little is known about his life beyond his writings on medicine. Hippocrates lived in the 400s BCE on the Greek island of Cos. There, he taught and practiced medicine.

Hippocrates is often credited with the four humors theory. Greeks believed the body had four humors. These were fluids called yellow bile, black bile, phlegm, and blood. The Greeks believed these humors could get out of balance, which caused illness. This is one of the first theories that focused on a cause of illness that wasn't religious or supernatural.

Hippocrates believed if doctors could find the cause of a sickness, then they could find a cure. So, he focused on patient examination. He asked his patients questions about their histories and **symptoms**. He found out as much as he could before making a **diagnosis**. This is called *clinical observation* and it is still used by doctors today.

Hippocrates

BORN: 460 BCE, island of Cos, Greece

DIED: around 375 BCE, Larissa, Thessaly

FACT: Hippocrates was an ancient Greek doctor.

FACT: Hippocrates is known as the Father of Medicine.

ACHIEVEMENTS

▶ Hippocrates focused on natural causes for diseases rather than supernatural or religious causes.

▶ Hippocrates developed and used methods doctors still use today, such as examining patients and asking questions about histories and **symptoms**.

▶ The Hippocratic Oath was named after Hippocrates. This is an oath that doctors take as a promise to practice medicine ethically.

STEM Star

CHAPTER 3

Pain-Free Surgery

Medical knowledge continued to advance from Hippocrates's time through the Roman Empire. But few new scientific discoveries were made during the **Middle Ages**. At that time, the Christian church was very powerful. Church leaders encouraged people to rely on faith rather than learning. These leaders spread the belief that disease was a punishment for sin. They said it could only be cured through prayer.

After the Middle Ages, scientific exploration started up again. Doctors learned a lot about the human body, especially the organs and blood. Surgery also became more common. But this was mainly sewing up wounds.

Prior to the 1800s, surgery was extremely risky. It often caused **infection** and pain. Procedures inside the body were very uncommon. Deeper surgical procedures became more common with the invention of anesthesia. This is used to **numb** patients or put them to sleep. Then they don't feel the pain of surgery.

In 1846, William Morton and John Warren performed the first successful procedure using anesthesia. They removed a **tumor** from a man's neck at Massachusetts General Hospital. Morton used ether to anesthetize the patient. Once the patient was unconscious, John Warren performed the surgery.

Ether, chloroform, and nitrous oxide were common forms of anesthesia. Patients could have surgery without experiencing severe pain. But dangers still existed. Doctors still didn't know that bacteria caused disease. So, they often didn't clean tools or operating rooms. Many people died of **infection** after surgery.

While surgery often wasn't successful, many different tools were used in the 1700s. These included knives, scalpels, needles, clamps, and more.

CHAPTER 4

Germ Theory

A major medical advancement came in the mid-1800s. That is when several scientists developed germ theory. This is the idea that diseases are caused by tiny organisms that can't be seen by the human eye. Germ theory led to discoveries of viruses and other organisms that caused illness.

One of the germ theory scientists was French biologist Louis Pasteur. He was working on improving alcoholic drinks such as beer and wine. Pasteur discovered that small living organisms caused these drinks to go sour. These organisms were bacteria that lived in the air. Pasteur believed these bacteria could also cause disease in humans.

Germ theory paved the way for safer surgery. British doctor Joseph Lister further advanced germ theory in the 1860s. Lister wanted to keep bacteria from entering wounds and causing **infection**. In 1865, he began spraying his surgical tools and bandages with an antiseptic. This is a chemical that kills bacteria. Over the next four years, deaths of Lister's patients after surgery fell from 45 percent to 15 percent!

Using antiseptics allowed doctors to perform procedures that were unsuccessful or even impossible before. Surgeons became skilled in operations inside the body. The first open-heart surgery took place in 1893.

New inventions made surgeries easier. German scientist Wilhelm Roentgen discovered x-rays in 1895. Doctors could use x-ray images to see inside the human body. Surgeons soon used x-rays to locate bullets inside soldiers and to perform other surgeries.

Louis Pasteur went on to develop vaccines for several illnesses, including rabies.

Anesthesia:
PAST AND PRESENT

Anesthesia methods have changed a lot in the past 100 years. The first anesthesiologists placed a cloth-covered mask over the patient's nose and mouth. Then they dripped the anesthetic onto it. Today's anesthesiologists use complicated machines. The machines monitor the patient's breathing and heart rate as well as administer the anesthetic.

ETHER OR CHLOROFORM

ETHER OR CHLOROFORM

DOSAGE BOTTLE

CARRYING POUCH

SCHIMMELBUSCH MASK

ANESTHESIA MACHINE

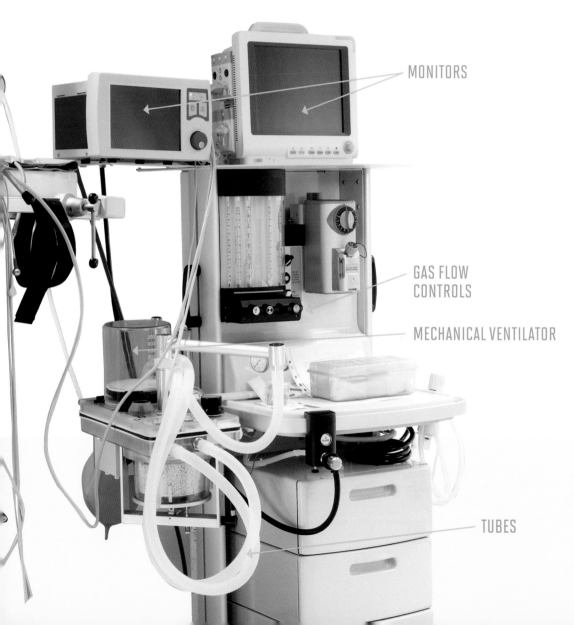

MONITORS

GAS FLOW CONTROLS

MECHANICAL VENTILATOR

TUBES

CHAPTER 5

Vaccines and Antibiotics

Once it was known that bacteria and viruses caused disease, scientists worked to develop treatments. They also looked for ways to prevent illness altogether. This led to the development of antibiotics and vaccines.

Antibiotics are used to cure illnesses caused by bacteria. One of the first antibiotics was penicillin. In 1928, British scientist Alexander Fleming was studying bacteria. He discovered mold growing on one of his bacteria samples.

When Fleming looked closely, he noticed that some bacteria near the mold were dying. Fleming grew more mold and discovered that it could kill many bacteria that caused disease. He named the substance penicillin. After further testing, penicillin was made widely **available**. It soon became the most popular and effective antibiotic on the market.

Antibiotics provided cures for diseases caused by bacteria. However, they don't work on diseases caused by viruses. Viruses are treated with vaccines.

Alexander Fleming was awarded the Nobel Prize in Physiology or Medicine for his discovery of penicillin.

Vaccines are made from weakened or dead viruses that cause disease. The virus in the vaccine isn't strong enough to cause disease. However, the body recognizes the virus and creates antibodies to fight it. The antibodies can then fight the disease-causing virus if a living **version** of it enters the body later! This is called an immune response.

By the 1920s, vaccines for tetanus, whooping cough, and other common illnesses were widely **available**. But other serious illnesses still existed without effective cures or treatments. One of the most feared illnesses at the time was polio. Polio can cause **paralysis** and death. Between 1894 and 1952, more than 80,000 people in the US were **infected** with the polio virus. Most of them were children.

Researchers began trying to develop a polio vaccine in the 1930s. But more than 15 years passed without success. Then American doctor and researcher Jonas Salk found the answer. He was able to create a vaccine from dead polio virus cells. Salk's vaccine was released in 1955. Over the next two years, the incidence of polio fell by more than 85 percent in the US. Today, the disease is only found in the countries Afghanistan, Pakistan, and Nigeria.

Jonas Salk

BORN: October 28, 1914, New York, New York

DIED: June 23, 1995, La Jolla, California

FACT: Salk received a medical degree from New York University in 1939.

FACT: Before working on the polio vaccine, Salk worked on developing a vaccine for **influenza**.

FACT: Salk became head of the Virus Research Laboratory at the University of Pittsburgh School of Medicine in 1947.

ACHIEVEMENTS

▶ Salk developed the first and most effective polio vaccine.

▶ In 1963 he became director of the Institute for Biological Studies in San Diego, California. It was later renamed the Salk Institute.

▶ Salk received the Presidential Medal of Freedom in 1977.

STEM Star

CHAPTER 6

Organ Transplants

By the late-1900s, people knew what caused most illnesses. These illnesses were often treated with medicines such as antibiotics or prevented altogether with vaccines. Surgery was also much safer. But attempts at **transplanting** organs had not been very successful. In the early 1900s, several doctors performed **kidney** transplants on both humans and animals. None of the transplanted organs worked for more than a few days.

Then, the first successful kidney transplant occurred in Boston, Massachusetts, in 1954. Richard Herrick received a kidney from his twin brother, Ronald. Other transplants soon followed.

Still, transplant success was limited. The main reason for this lack of success is that the receiving body often rejects the donor organ. This is when the person's immune system reacts to the new organ as if it's a virus or other danger. The immune system fights the new organ, causing the organ to fail.

Organ transplant outcomes improved dramatically with the invention of the drug Cyclosporine. Belgian researcher Jean Borel

A blood collection program began in the United States in the 1940s. Today, blood drives are commonly held in schools, offices, and collection centers to encourage people to give blood.

discovered it in the 1970s. Cyclosporine weakens the body's immune system so it won't fight against new organs.

Cyclosporine was approved for commercial use in 1983. The drug remains one of the most successful anti-rejection medicines today. There are still more people in need of organ **transplants** than there are donors. But scientists are hopeful that new **technologies** will lead to more transplants and longer lives.

CHAPTER 7

Preventive Medicine

The medical field has changed more than almost any industry. Medical methods and **technologies** get safer and more effective every year. The medical field has also become increasingly **specialized**. While there are still many general doctors, many others specialize in a particular field. For example, a doctor may specialize in children's health or heart disease.

One important modern medical specialty is preventive medicine. This kind of medicine focuses on preventing illness and helping people live healthier lives. This includes reducing risky behaviors, eating a more healthful diet, exercising, and more. While preventive medicine is a specialty, all doctors help their patients prevent illness and make healthy choices.

Preventive medicine has created some of the most important advancements in modern medicine. One of these is education on the risks of smoking. Cigarette smoke is considered one of the main causes of preventable diseases in the United States. These diseases include certain **cancers** and heart disease.

In the 1970s and 1980s, cities and states began limiting where people could smoke in public places. Today, smoking is banned in most businesses, restaurants, and more.

The first major studies on the effects of smoking occurred in the 1950s. But it wasn't until 1964 that the Surgeon General of the United States Health Service admitted the connection between smoking and disease. Since then, doctors and other organizations have focused on preventing people from starting smoking and helping people to quit smoking.

In 1965, 42 percent of US adults smoked. In 2015, that number was just 15 percent. Reducing the number of smokers reduced the number of deaths related to cigarette smoking.

CHAPTER 8

Fatal Disease

While preventive medicine is very helpful, it can't stop every disease or illness. And unfortunately, not all diseases have cures. One fatal disease is **cancer**. No one has found a cure for it yet. But new treatments are constantly being developed. Doctors must stay up-to-date on the latest tools and treatments in order to help their patients.

Today, doctors and surgeons have advanced tools to look inside the body. These include CT and PET scans, MRIs, and ultrasounds. Such tools can find cancer cells and **tumors**. Once found, cancer is treated with a combination of drugs, **radiation**, and surgery.

Another often fatal disease is human immunodeficiency virus (HIV). This is a virus that attacks the body's immune system. People with HIV often develop acquired immune deficiency syndrome (AIDS). HIV and AIDS were a leading cause of death in the 1990s. There was little that doctors could do.

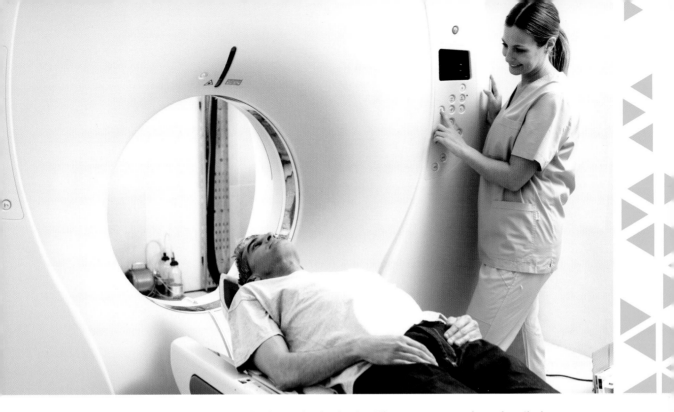

CT scans use x-rays to look inside the body. These scans produce detailed images. CT scans are often used to look at the brain, neck, stomach, and chest.

There is still no cure for HIV and AIDS, but there are better treatments. People with HIV or AIDS are treated with antiretroviral drugs. These drugs don't cure the virus, but they slow its spread. HIV and AIDS patients can now live longer lives.

While there are no cures for fatal diseases, treatments can help extend patients' lives. Researchers hope to find cures for **cancer** and AIDS. With new **technologies** and advancements every day, a healthier future is possible.

CHAPTER 9

The Future of Medicine

Many new medical technologies are being developed today that will change the future of medicine. One new **technology** is robotic surgery. This is surgery performed or assisted by a robot!

Most surgical robots have camera arms to view the area being operated on. These robots also have mechanical arms to perform procedures. Often, robots can work in small spaces and on hard-to-reach areas more easily than surgeons. They can also be steadier and more precise than surgeons.

In 2016, researchers in Washington, DC, conducted a study with the Smart Tissue **Autonomous** Robot (STAR). They compared its performance to that of a human surgeon. The researchers found that STAR's work was neater and more effective.

Another important technology is artificial body parts. Scientists have produced artificial limbs as well as artificial organs, including hearts. Researchers are also working to produce artificial blood.

3-D printing can be used to make artificial limbs. This is helpful for children who outgrow replacement limbs and need new ones.

This blood could be used to make blood cells to treat illnesses. It could also be used for transfusions. This is when someone's blood is removed and replaced with new blood. Patients who have blood diseases often receive healthy blood through transfusions.

Drugs and **technologies** developed by doctors and scientists of the past have changed the face of medicine. Today's medical researchers will continue to work on curing diseases and helping people live healthier lives. Medicine will likely continue to advance at a rapid pace!

Timeline

400s BCE — Hippocrates develops methods of clinical observation and teaches and practices medicine.

500–1500 CE — Few new scientific discoveries are made because church leaders encourage people to rely on faith rather than learning.

1846 — William Morton and John Warren perform the first successful procedure using anesthesia.

mid-1800s — Germ theory is developed by Louis Pasteur and other scientists.

1865 — Joseph Lister begins spraying his surgical tools and bandages with an antiseptic.

1928 Alexander Fleming creates penicillin.

1955 Jonas Salk's polio vaccine is released.

1964 The Surgeon General of the United States Health Service publishes a report about the connection between smoking and disease.

1983 Jean Borel's anti-rejection medicine cyclosporine is approved for use in transplant patients.

2016 A study shows that the Smart Tissue Autonomous Robot (STAR) performs better than a human surgeon.

Glossary

autonomous—having the power or ability to make decisions and act independently.

available—able to be had or used.

cancer—any of a group of often deadly diseases marked by harmful changes in the normal growth of cells. Cancer can spread and destroy healthy tissues and organs.

diagnosis—the act of identifying a disease, illness, or problem by examining someone or something.

infection—an unhealthy condition caused by something harmful, such as bacteria. If something has an infection, it is infected.

influenza—a common illness that is caused by a virus and that causes fever, weakness, severe aches and pains, and breathing problems.

kidney—one of a pair of organs that help the body get rid of waste products.

Middle Ages—a period in European history that lasted from about 500 CE to about 1500 CE.

numb—to make someone unable to feel pain or touch.

paralysis—the loss of motion or feeling in a part of the body.

radiation—the use of controlled amounts of x-rays for the treatment of diseases such as cancer.

specialize—to pursue one branch of study or type of work, called a specialty.

symptom—a noticeable change in the normal working of the body. A symptom indicates or accompanies disease, sickness, or other malfunction.

technology (tehk-NAH-luh-jee)—machinery and equipment developed for practical purposes using scientific principles and engineering.

transplant—to surgically move an organ from one body to another.

tumor—an abnormal mass of cells in the body.

version—a different form or type of an original.

Online Resources

Booklinks
NONFICTION NETWORK
FREE! ONLINE NONFICTION RESOURCES

To learn more about medicine, visit **abdobooklinks.com**. These links are routinely monitored and updated to provide the most current information available.

Index